Do you know what an adjective is? Share your ideas.

Adjectives are AWESOME!
There's just no doubt about it.
They take a noun—any noun—
and tell us more about it.
These bugs will demonstrate for you
just what an adjective can do.

clean bug

An adjective is a word that describes a noun such as a bug. *Clean* and *mean* are both adjectives.

mean bug

Can you think of some other adjectives that describe these bugs?

gigantic, friendly, green bug

3

strong bug

long bug

annoying, tagalong bug

sticky bug

picky bug

speedy bug

greedy bug

Lots of adjectives end in the letter *y*. How many can you think of?

outrageous bug

contagious bug

Sometimes you can make an adjective out of a noun or verb by adding a special ending such as *-ic*, *-ous*, *-ish*, *-ful*, *-ing*, *-al*, or *-able*.

Example:
hero + ic = heroic
courage + ous = courageous

Try to make adjectives out of these words:
humor, beauty, love, fool, magic, forget, wish, frighten

heroic and courageous bug

silly bug

chilly bug

surprised bug

disguised bug

gymnastic bugs

elastic bugs

many enthusiastic bugs

Can you think of adjectives to describe each of these bugs?

When you want to modify a noun,
an adjective won't let you down.
Try adding adjectives—they're incredible
at making nouns UNFORGETTABLE!